WISLEY

A WELL-LOVED CENTRE FOR GARDENING EXCELLENCE

I am delighted to welcome you to the Royal Horticultural Society's Garden at Wisley. Every time I visit I marvel again at the diversity of the plants and features on offer through all the seasons of the year. In

any week, in any season the visitor is bound to find something in flower or of interest. Because of this great range, many people believe that there is not another garden in the world to equal it. There is the variety of the Rock Garden and the Alpine Houses, the trials in the Portsmouth Field, the mixed borders, the heather garden in Howard's Field, the ornamental glasshouses, the rhododendrons of Battleston Hill and much more. You will notice the continuing improvements to the Garden and its facilities. Enjoy the excellent shop and restaurant, and the plant centre with its outstanding selection. I am sure that many more people will wish to join the Royal Horticultural Society and share in the development of this magnificent Garden.

Sir Simon Hornby

PRESIDENT, RHS

◀ *Opposite:* In Seven Acres this tupelo, *Nyssa sylvatica*, radiates warmth and beauty

Cover: The Tudor-style Laboratory building from across the Canal

◀◀ **See Garden Plan, left (under flap)**

1 Conifer Lawn
2 Mixed Borders
3 Summer Garden/Garden for New Rose Introductions
4 Battleston Hill
5 Mediterranean Garden
6 Battleston East
7 Winter Garden
8 The Portsmouth Field
9 Jubilee Arboretum
10 Model Gardens
11 Glasshouses
12 Plant Demonstration Area and Refreshment Kiosk
13 Fruit Field
14 Model Fruit Gardens/Herb Garden
15 Weather Hill/Bowes Lyon Pavilion/ Rose Borders and Catenary
16 Alpine Display Houses/Model Vegetable Garden/Monocot Borders
17 Rock Garden/Alpine Meadow
18 Bowles' Corner
19 Laboratory Building/Canal and Loggia
20 Walled Gardens
21 Wild Garden
22 Seven Acres
23 Pinetum/Riverside Walk
24 Howard's Field and Heather Garden

INTRODUCTION

The Garden of the Royal Horticultural Society at Wisley is a unique blend of the beautiful and the instructive. For over 90 years, it has been a source of inspiration, practical example and advice to members of the Society and it has become a mecca for gardeners and garden-lovers everywhere. The Alpine Meadow, carpeted with wild daffodils in spring, and Battleston Hill, brilliant with rhododendrons in early summer, are just two features for which the Garden is famous. There are many others: the Rock Garden, jewelled with flowers in April and May, contrasts with the cooler attractions of the Wild Garden and its long succession of plants; the Mixed Borders and Rose Gardens are ablaze with colour from high summer into autumn, when the Fruit Field and Model Fruit Gardens reach their most productive; and the trees and shrubs of Seven Acres put on a fine winter display, while the Glasshouses offer shelter to both plants and people throughout each and every season.

The Royal Horticultural Society came to Wisley in 1904, although at that time only a small part of the 24-ha (60-acre) estate was actually cultivated as a garden, the remainder being wooded farmland. The original garden was the creation of George Ferguson Wilson – businessman, scientist, inventor and keen gardener and a former Treasurer of the Society. In 1878, he purchased the site and established the 'Oakwood experimental garden', with the idea of making 'difficult plants grow successfully'. His hopes were so amply fulfilled that the garden soon became renowned for its collections of lilies, gentians, Japanese irises, primulas and water plants, all looking at home in an informal woodland setting. The present Wild Garden at Wisley is the direct descendant of 'Oakwood' and, despite great changes since Wilson's day, is still true to his concept.

Oakwood and the adjoining Glebe Farm were then bought by Sir Thomas Hanbury, a wealthy Quaker who had founded the celebrated garden of La Mortola, on the Italian Riviera, with which the RHS remains closely concerned. In 1903, Sir Thomas presented the Wisley estate in trust to the Royal Horticultural Society, for its perpetual use.

Nothing could have been more providential. For at least 30

years, the Society had been seeking a larger garden 'beyond the radius of the London smoke', to replace the garden at Chiswick which it had leased since 1822. It was also committed to building a new exhibition hall and offices at Vincent Square, Westminster. At a stroke, Sir Thomas's generous donation made it all possible. By May 1904, the move from Chiswick to Wisley was complete and, in July, the new headquarters at Vincent Square, Westminster, were officially opened by King Edward VII – both in time to mark the centenary.

Over 6,000 people visited Wisley during its first year under the Society's control and those who criticised its inaccessible position were quickly silenced by 'the great development of road traction'. Others considered the situation and soil most unsuitable. The latter is naturally acid sand, which is poor in nutrients and fast draining, although in places well supplied with water. Lying in the valley of the River Wey, the Garden is vulnerable to frequent harsh frosts, often continuing into May and early June, and it is also exposed to biting northeast winds. Wisley has been hit by freak weather on several occasions. In June 1947 a violent storm caused severe flooding (in 'the Temperate House Fellows had to crowd for safety on the centre bench'); in July 1965, a tornado devastated the Fruit Field; in October 1987 and January 1990, the great storms which swept across Britain resulted in the loss of hundreds of trees, leaving a trail of destruction on Battleston Hill, in the Wild Garden and the Pinetum. Growing conditions at Wisley are certainly not easy, but in this respect it is an ideal testing ground for plants: if they succeed here, they will (except for lime-hating plants) have a good chance of succeeding almost anywhere in Britain.

A trials field committee judging a potato trial in the Portsmouth Field. For visitors, the trials offer a rare opportunity to see an unrivalled collection of cultivars of a particular plant and to compare, assess or simply admire them

At this time rock gardening was very much in fashion and the construction of the Rock Garden was the Society's first major undertaking, in 1911. Other areas were already being developed: the somewhat overgrown Wild Garden was cleared, a range of glasshouses was erected, Seven Acres, the Pinetum and Howard's Field were planted and the rose borders were established on Weather Hill. Wisley was taking shape as an ornamental garden, but its educational and scientific roles were never forgotten. A small laboratory was opened, later to be incorporated in the romantic, half-timbered, Tudor-style building of 1916; the School of Horticulture was founded; and the trials of flowers, vegetables and fruit, which have been such an important part of the Society's work since 1860, were resumed and expanded.

Today the Laboratory building houses the administrative staff and advisory officers of the Society. The latter provide a valuable service for members, answering thousands of queries on plant identification, pests and diseases, soil improvement and general gardening problems. Both scientific and garden staff give talks, hold demonstrations of techniques such as planting, pruning and propagation and conduct garden walks. Staff collect seed in the Garden each year and over 200,000 packets of clean and identified seed are sent all over the world every year under the Society's surplus seed distribution scheme. Scientific investigation and horticultural research are also carried out on a regular basis.

The World Wars affected Wisley, as elsewhere. During the First World War, the Director, Professor Keeble, became head of the Food Production Department, Ministry of Agriculture, one of many changes, and after the war more women were employed in the Garden. In the Second World War, some shows continued to be held, and the more valuable books from the Lindley Library were stored at Wisley. The first model garden was constructed – an Allotment Garden. It may have been war, but in a little known war-time project, the RHS sent vegetable and flower seeds and bulbs to Prisoner of War camps in Germany and Italy. Even more astonishing, it was recorded in February 1943 that 'nine candidates from the Prisoner of War Camp Stalag XXA, recently sat for the Society's General Examination (Seniors). . . .' Five passed.

The Society is actively involved in running horticultural training programmes and organising examinations. A School of Horticulture was set up in 1907 to instruct young people in the principles of horticulture and prepare them for careers as professional gardeners, continuing the Society's traditional responsibilities for horticultural education, stretching back to the 1820s when 'labourers' were invited to train at the Chiswick garden. Among those early student gardeners were Joseph Paxton, later knighted for designing the Crystal Palace, and the great plant-hunter, Robert Fortune. Since then, many leading horticulturists have benefited from the School of Horticulture. The one-year programme is an integrated part of other schemes of horticultural education.

The RHS is the leading international trials institution and the main trials ground here at Wisley is the Portsmouth Field, which occupies about 1.5 ha (4 acres). It accommodates all the trials, apart from those of woody plants, rock plants and of tender plants under glass. The trials of ornamental plants and vegetable 'epitomise . . . the Society's endeavour to show to the public the best kinds of plants to grow' and have always been one of the principal objects of the Garden. That combination of learning with pleasure is the essence of Wisley itself.

There is also a mostly secret world of wildlife here at Wisley. Up to 144 species of birds have been recorded, as many as 90 regularly, and a number can be observed, especially when rearing young, at quiet times and in the winter months. There are mammals too, some more welcome than others, squirrels and rabbits, badgers and mink, and foxes and deer. Dedicated staff record birds, put up nest boxes and keep hives for bees.

The present Garden occupies approximately 97 ha (240 acres) and the number of visitors each year is approaching 750,000. Like any garden, Wisley is a dynamic place: the devastating storms acted as a facelift, speeding up the pace of change and giving scope to rethink and redevelop major areas. We can be sure that Wisley Garden will retain its unique character and charm and remain a centre for gardening excellence.

Since the end of the First World War, women have formed a significant group at Wisley. About half of the staff and the 30 or so trainee gardeners are now women

5

STROLLING AROUND WISLEY GARDEN

Such is the richness of horticulture on view in the Garden, it is helpful to plan a route, according to time and energy. This guide presents two main walks in the central area of the Garden, each quite different in feel. The first walk suggests innumerable ideas and gives instruction in an unusually wide range of horticultural subjects. The second walk is calmer, views are open, yet wooded. This is a more introspective Wisley.

Whichever way you choose to walk, simply enjoy the beauty and peace of this extraordinary garden.

1 A Walk to Inspire Gardeners (page 8)
Conifer Lawn
Mixed Borders
Summer Garden / Garden for New Rose Introductions
Battleston Hill / Mediterranean Garden
Model Gardens / Glasshouses
Weather Hill / Rose Catenary
Alpine Display Houses / Model Vegetable Garden /
     Monocot Borders
Rock Garden / Alpine Meadow
Memorial Water Feature and Bowles' Corner

Bonus Walks: Battleston East / Winter Garden
                 Portsmouth Field
                 Jubilee Arboretum
                 Fruit Field

2 Semi-Woodland Walk (page 43)
Laboratory and Canal
Formal Garden / Walled Garden
Wild Garden
Seven Acres / Round Pond / Lake

Bonus Walks: Riverside Walk
                 Pinetum
                 Howard's Field and Heather Garden

Bonus Walks

By including a Bonus Walk, your visit can be extended by perhaps half an hour (**L**) or more than an hour (**LL**). These quiet and less crowded outer reaches of the Garden are sometimes over-looked, but each has much to offer. Plan to include at least one in each visit to enjoy all that the Garden has to offer.

During your walks, refer to the map inside the front cover.

ENTRANCE

On entering the Garden immediately ahead on your right is a massive oak tree, between 210-220 years old, which has welcomed visitors to Wisley Garden from the earliest days. Branches have naturally grafted themselves together, often a sign of pollarding in the past. Look for the resulting two large circled or looped branches, which fascinate children. In the shade of the old oak tree can be found a selection of *Hosta, Hemerocallis* and *Geranium* interplanted amongst winter-flowering *Viburnum* and hardy summer-flowering fuchsias. Just beside it is the little gatehouse where, until 1962, a uniformed Gate Attendant requested that everyone sign the Visitors' Book.

In August, the orange flowers of the trumpet vine, *Campsis* × *tagliabuana* 'Madame Galen', enjoy the warm west wall of the Laboratory

Passing through the gates to Wisley is like stepping back in time, to a leisured age of large private gardens and spacious lawns. However, these imposing wrought-iron gates, emblazoned with the date of the Society's founding in 1804, leave no doubt that this is an RHS Garden. The gates commemorate the Reverend William Wilks. To him we owe the well-known Shirley poppies. Look for these poppies in the gate design.

To your right is the focal point of the Garden, the country-house style building known as the Laboratory. It looks much older than it is, in part because it was built from 1914-16 of materials recycled from old manor houses around the district. Stop to admire the border along the south wall on your right. Here, early in the year, you can see the rich double yellow flowers of *Jasminum mesnyi*, brought from China by Robert Fortune, followed later by the white scented flowers of the tender *Buddleja asiatica*. The bright yellow *Rosa* 'Helen Knight' was raised in 1966 by the then Director using seed of *R. ecae*, which grew on the wall of his house at Wisley. It caused a sensation and was soon in the nursery catalogues. The dry, sunny bed below is appreciated by a host of bulbous plants, including the summer-flowering *Crinum* × *powellii* 'Cape Dawn'. Along the warm west wall of the building, the orange flowers of the trumpet vine, *Campsis* × *tagliabuana* 'Madame Galen', are a gorgeous sight in August.

Directly ahead is the Wright Memorial Sundial. The first Superintendent, Samuel T. Wright, supervised the move from Chiswick and remained at Wisley until his death. On the left is the Garden House where he lived for 18 years. The sandstone walls provide a congenial home for white candytuft, gold dust, aubrieta, and other crevice-loving plants.

Leave the Laboratory building for now. You may look at the front of the building on your return walk or at the beginning of the Semi-Woodland Walk (page 43).

A Walk to Inspire Gardeners

There are two paths before you. The path on the left leads up the steps to the Terrace and the Mixed Borders (page 9). The path on the right leads to the Conifer Lawn from which you can also easily reach the Broad Walk of the Mixed Borders.

1

CONIFER LAWN

Between the Terrace and the 'Canal' is the Conifer Lawn, a tranquil area with remnants of a small pinetum on gentle lawns. This early area of the Garden, where many more conifers once stood, boasts a Chilean incense cedar, *Austrocedrus (Libocedrus) chilensis*, one of the tallest in Britain at over 17.5m (58ft) , and a rare *Juniperus monosperma*, with feathery foliage. The border along the lawn contains some fine Japanese maples and one or two old roses. With your back to the Laboratory building, turn left to the Terrace to join the Mixed Borders.

2

MIXED BORDERS

Above: The stately Conifer Lawn and the Laboratory building beyond recall a more leisured age. *Below:* The unrivalled Mixed Borders contain all the traditional perennials.

Cross the Terrace – a wide path with lawns dotted with circular and oblong beds of spring and summer bedding plants each side – to the Mixed Borders. They are chief among the glories of Wisley, and each is 128 m long by 6m wide (420 by 20ft). You can see them rise gently towards Battleston Hill, backed by hornbeam hedges and with a wide grass walk between them, the Broad Walk. All the traditional perennials are here – border phlox, geraniums, coreopsis, agapanthus, red hot pokers, monkshoods, Japanese anemones, and, of course, peonies, chrysanthemums and Michaelmas daisies.

The borders provide the visitor with a spectacle rich in herbaceous plants, with shrubs to provide a framework and bulbs for interplanting. Composition is all, achieved through graded colour schemes, and variations in textures and height. The period of interest extends well beyond summer to includce newly emerging foliage in spring, and frost-encrusted leaves and skeletal stems of winter.

Near the Terrace on the right-hand side running at right angles to the Mixed Borders, and towards Weather Hill, is an entrance to the Summer Garden.

SUMMER GARDEN

This garden features plants flowering from June onwards and demonstrates various colour combinations which could be used in a small garden. The quarter-circle beds round a central urn contain seasonal bedding plants. Shrub roses and hardy

fuchsias in other beds are set off by a medley of aquilegias, salvias, sedums, bellflowers, day lilies, potentillas, agapanthus, irises, red hot pokers and geraniums. *Artemisia* 'Powis Castle' forms a silvery clump in one corner and there is a fine example of the tree peony, *Paeonia suffruticosa* 'Rock's Variety'.

The west of the Summer Garden is bounded by roses trained along post and wire fences. They include the long-flowering, sweet-scented Musk roses, 'Buff Beauty' and 'Cornelia', with apricot-yellow and coppery pink blooms, the ever-popular, thornless Bourbon rose, 'Zéphirine Drouhin', in cerise pink, and some of the vigorous, prickly Penzance briers, with apple-scented foliage, dating from the end of the 19th century but now seldom grown.

From June onwards the Summer Garden is a particular delight. Many of the planting schemes here are suitable for a small garden

The Autumn Borders are also on the right of the Broad Walk, between the Summer Garden and the Garden for New Rose Introductions. Designed for late summer and autumn colour, in these two smaller borders Korean chrysanthemums and perennial asters are to the fore. Once the autumn frosts are with us the stools of the Korean chrysanthemums are lifted and kept cool and dry in the propagation department until early spring. These are richly supplemented with the violet-flowered *Liriope muscari* and *Sedum spectabile* – with flat heads of rosy-pink flowers attracting late butterflies and other insects.

GARDEN FOR NEW ROSE INTRODUCTIONS

The garden lies to the right of the main Mixed Borders and above the Summer Garden. Over 200 cultivars of bush and pillar rose introduced during the previous ten years are on view and the garden is topped up annually with introductions from the current year. Once past the ten-year limit, the roses are either planted elsewhere at Wisley or discarded. Each year a section of the soil is sterilised to prevent it becoming 'rose sick' before the latest additions are planted.

Deer are not encouraged anywhere in the garden, and here they can do much damage. One night these uninvited guests

The Garden for New Rose Introductions displays over 200 cultivars of bush and pillar rose. This collection comprises roses that have been introduced in the past ten years and new introductions are added every year

ate every single bloom of *Rosa* 'Iceberg', rejecting all other varieties on offer.

A leaflet listing the roses in this section and giving addresses of suppliers is available from the Reception in the Laboratory building.

To complete A Walk to Inspire Gardeners, rejoin the Mixed Borders and then the Terrace. (You can leave by a small exit from Mixed Borders directly into the Plant Sales area, although there is no readmission from this point.)

BATTLESTON HILL

Broad Walk

The Broad Walk is the path between the long Mixed Borders which continues up into Battleston Hill, a high wooded ridge running from east to west and falling away on the side of the Portsmouth Field and the A3 road. The gardens here, especially of Battleston East on the left, are much more extensive than they first appear and a visit in May and June, when the azaleas and rhododendrons are in bloom, is an unforgettable experience.

Staying on the Broad Walk, look for the hardy hybrid rhododendrons (what might be thought of as the 'typical' rhododendron) to the left of the Broad Walk up the hill. This is a showcase for many excellent cultivars which have received awards from the Society.

To the right of the main walk are evergreen hybrid azaleas, largely derived from *R. kaempferi*. Prominent among them are the Kurume azaleas, introduced in 1918 from a Japanese nursery by the famous plant collector, E H Wilson, and considered by him to be 'the loveliest of all Azaleas'.

Although rhododendrons are the stars of Battleston Hill, there is much else to ensure variety and prolong the season of interest. Camellias and magnolias open the year; among them are many *Camellia japonica* cultivars.

The lilies scattered throughout the woodland are mostly hybrids, too numerous to mention. In summer they present an inviting and floriferous picture with fuchsias, hostas, day lilies, red hot pokers, astilbes and agapanthus. By the curving path at the foot of Battleston Hill are some of the hydrangeas, including the lovely forms of *H. paniculata*. In a damp patch on the corner, *Gunnera manicata* unfurls its enormous leaves amid a group of moisture-loving perennials that includes candelabra primulas and the umbrella plant, *Peltiphyllum peltatum*.

On the other side of the walk is a multi-coloured mass of *Tovara virginiana* 'Painter's Palette'.

This ever steeper Broad Walk takes you to the brow of the hill, the highest point at Wisley, from where it is possible to view large parts of the Garden and surrounding countryside. Here, too, is an collection of eucalyptus trees outstanding for their glaucous foliage and peeling bark, exposing multi-coloured trunks. Of particular note are the ghostly white stems of *E. urnigera* and the marbled trunks of *E. niphophila*. On the slope below is the Mediterranean Garden (page 14). The flight of wide curving steps, framed with weeping cherries, mark the transition point between Battleston Hill and the Portsmouth Field (page 16).

Return back along the Broad Walk, turning left at the surfaced road to go to the Model Gardens (page 19).

OR, for a more extensive walk, with your back to the brow of the hill, turn right along any path off the Broad Walk to Battleston East (page 14) and the Winter Garden (page 16).

Battleston Hill sweeps upwards with rhododendrons, evergreen hybrid azaleas, lilies and much else on either side

MEDITERRANEAN GARDEN

In the hottest part of the Garden, on the slope down from the top of the Broad Walk to the Portsmouth Field below, a feature has been developed which can be loosely described as the Mediterranean Garden. The steepest part of this dry south-facing slope has been terraced with railway sleepers. This area contains many sun-loving plants from the Mediterranean, Australasia, California and some hardy South African plants. Included in the planting scheme are *Ceanothus, Cytisus, Salvia* and *Eucalyptus*, as well as herbaceous plants and bulbs for different seasons.

BATTLESTON EAST

You will be spoilt for choice among the charming circulatory paths, leading downwards to the Winter Garden, the Portsmouth Field, and eventually to the steps up through the Mediterranean Garden to the brow of Battleston Hill, completing a varied and interesting circular route back to the Mixed Borders.

Battleston Hill has been transformed since the storms of 1987 and 1990 which did so much damage to the woodland and mature trees that formed a major part of this area. Battleston East experienced most change and is now much more accessible with solid paths or wood chipped paths. The shelter belts which formed Battleston Hill's initial plantings are gradually being thinned so as to allow those remaining to become specimen trees.

Rhododendrons, which provide the major display for about four months of the year, are being augmented by many other fine plants. In January and February, *Hamamelis* and *Sarcococca* fill the air with their fragrance and display their spidery flowers. March and April bring displays of camellias; firstly *Camellia* × *williamsii* hybrids soon followed by *C. japonica*.

A large number of magnolias supplement the floral display starting with *M. campbellii* forms in February and March and continuing through to the strongly scented *M. hypoleuca* seen in midsummer.

Herbaceous plants provide additional interest during the summer, ranging from primulas and hostas through the large collection of lilies, which continue well into August. In autumn, fruits and foliage provide colour which, if birds allow, will retain their fruit well into the New Year. There are many birds in this area, which on a quiet winter's day scold visitors who dare to disturb their idyllic territory. Large plantings of evergreen azaleas can be seen from the Garden's approach road, providing quite a variation in foliage colour throughout the autumn and winter.

It is also a favourite spot for wildlife. One night a group of staff were quietly observing a badger sett in the moonlight, when they were delighted to find fox cubs playing around their feet.

At the bottom of the slope here, Battleston East merges with the Winter Garden.

The gardens of Battleston East and Battleston West are extensive and most deserving of a special visit, especially in May and June when the azaleas and rhododendrons, here *R.* 'Red Carpet' on Battleston West, provide a spectacle

WINTER GARDEN

This strip of woodland at the eastern end of the Portsmouth Field has been carefully planted to be at its best between November and March. Daphnes, viburnums, mahonias, winter sweet, heathers, Chinese witch hazel and *Prunus subhirtella* 'Autumnalis' enliven the bleakest months with their blossom, often deliciously fragrant as a bonus. The gaily coloured berries of *Pernettya mucronata* 'Winter Time' persist through winter, as do the crab apples of *Malus* × *robusta*. The snaky-striped bark of *Acer grosseri* var. *hersii* seems particularly conspicuous then.

Return to the Mixed Borders to continue A Walk to Inspire Gardeners by crossing the Portsmouth Field to the steps which lead up to the top of Battleston Hill, the Mixed Borders and the Model Gardens (page 19).

OR, for a much longer walk, after looking around the Portsmouth Field, continue on to the far side of the Field to the Jubilee Arboretum.

THE PORTSMOUTH FIELD

The gently sloping Portsmouth Field is the main trials area of Wisley where plants are grown specifically for the purpose of comparing the different cultivars available and assessing their merits. Trials are of two types – permanent and invited. Permanent trials, which continue from year to year, include delphiniums, dahlias, chrysanthemums and sweet peas.

Invited trials, of selected crops which change each year, concentrate on annual and biennial flowers, plus some perennials, and vegetables, and also pot plants in the Glasshouses. These trials are open to everyone – amateur gardeners, whether members of the RHS or not, and professional seedsmen – who are 'invited' to submit seeds or plants from the calendar of trials

which appears in the RHS Journal, *The Garden*, each autumn.

Trials entries raised from seed are normally grown under number and cultivar name, and a detailed record of their growth is kept by the Trials Department. Information boards, detailing entries, cultivation processes and award recommendations, are displayed adjacent to each trial.

All plants are inspected by the appropriate committees of the Society, who can often be observed carrying out their pleasant but very necessary duties. Based on their recommendations the prestigious Award of Garden Merit may be given. A full report of most trials is available and descriptions of award-winning plants are published in the Society's *Proceedings*. The trials are regularly listed in *The Garden* and *Newsletter*.

The trials are one of the most important aspects of the work of the Garden. There is nothing quite like the sight of the Portsmouth Field in summer and especially striking is the trial of delphiniums standing tall and stately in a variety of blues, whites and pinks. Return to Battleston Hill and the Mixed Borders via the steps up through the Mediterranean Garden.

OR, leaving the trials ground on the way to the Jubilee Arboretum (page 18), note the superb specimen of the rare big cone pine, *Pinus coulteri*, which is distinguished by its remarkably large cones and spreading bunches of leaves each like a chimney-sweep's brush.

The Portsmouth Field (*above*): committee members assess the permanent delphinium trial, a striking sight in summer. *Below*: Carrot trials

JUBILEE ARBORETUM

ll The Jubilee Arboretum covers some 13 ha (32 acres) of undulating land around the Fruit Field and was developed to mark the Silver Jubilee of Queen Elizabeth II. It was opened on 8 May 1978 by Her Majesty and HRH Prince Philip, who planted the first two trees – a pair of upright purple beeches, *Fagus sylvatica* 'Dawyck Purple'. (That year was also the centenary of the first plantings at Wisley by G F Wilson.) A columnar English oak, *Quercus robur* 'Fastigiata', was the third tree to be planted, at the end of the broad lime avenue into the Arboretum; it commemorates Bert Pullinger, who worked here for over half a century. Many of the trees were donated by the Hampshire-based Hillier Nurseries, when forced to reduce its enormous range of trees and shrubs, and the Society owes much to the generosity of the late Sir Harold Hillier. Although the main planting is now complete, a good deal of infilling with trees and complementary shrubs is on-going. A series of grassland rides directs visitors to important features.

Populus × canadensis 'Serotina Aurea', one of hundreds of trees in the Jubilee Arboretum

The Arboretum, like Wisley itself, has been planted to combine beauty with education and has three major interwoven themes. The first groups trees according to their season of interest and, in this way, maintains a year-round display throughout the area. There is autumn colour, which can even be enjoyed by motorists passing by on the A3.

The second theme links trees on the basis of their common

characteristics, such as shape, colour and type of foliage and flowers. It has already been put into practice with weeping trees, columnar trees, including fastigate forms of oak, maple and *Ginkgo biloba*, and trees with variegated leaves and will be extended to separate sections for trees with coloured, aromatic and divided foliage and with scented flowers. This system of planting is not only ornamental, but extremely useful to ordinary gardeners faced with the task of choosing a tree for their own gardens. A range of trees sharing a particular attribute can be assessed on the spot and their habits and rates of growth compared, so much easier than studying trees in a nursery catalogue.

The third theme of the Arboretum is botanical, again helpful to gardeners. In this case, a small genus is selected and all its species and cultivars are planted together. Obviously, this is not feasible with a large genus like *Quercus*, numbering about 600 species, but with a small genus such as *Catalpa* it is both effective and instructive.

Informal plantings of shrubs are being added to the collection of trees with *Forsythia* and *Escallonia* giving spring and summer interest. These beds will enable the visitor to compare species and hybrids at close quarters and to assess the differences in flower, foliage and growth characteristics.

At any point in your walk around the Arboretum, you can cut up the hill to the Fruit Field (page 27). The central path there takes you to the back of the Glasshouses (refer to the map) to go to the Model Gardens.

10

MODEL GARDENS

Wisley, to many people, means the Model Gardens. Located between the Glasshouses and the rose borders of Weather Hill, they have been created specifically with the needs of the average gardener in mind and offer a host of ideas and practical suggestions. The Model Gardens are on either side of the path all the way to the Glasshouses, where they continue on the right-hand side.

A Garden for All Seasons demonstrates how much can be achieved in a small space; here the colourful planting includes *Carex elata* 'Aurea', *Salvia officinalis* 'Icterina', *Delphinium* 'Blue Heaven', *Hemerocallis* and lupin

The Garden for All Seasons

Early in 1991 this specialist garden was created as a companion to the Reader's Digest book of the same name. Its year-round theme, sumptuous planting and juxtaposing of styles has since proved it a popular addition to the Model Garden range.

The Town Garden

On the northern side of the path is a narrow town garden, 22 by 7 m (72 by 24 ft). Designed with simplicity and cost in mind, it is laid to grass with curved beds of summer bedding.

The Family Garden

The slightly larger garden next door, sponsored by Rolawn, meets the demands of family life with a patio, barbecue, children's play space, utility area and quiet sitting places.

The Enthusiast's Garden
Designed by Robin Williams and sponsored by Sainsbury's Homebase, this new garden pays attention to design and planting associations using a wide and varied range of plants.

Living Rooms Garden
Opposite is a garden designed by Ann Kennedy and sponsored by Agriframes in association with Barrett Homes. It shows how a garden can be divided by using wall plants and climbers attached to vertical supports, and interlinking water features.

Container Garden
Next on the south side is an exciting display of patio pots and containers. Some are planted with trees, shrubs and other perennials, while others change with seasons, brimming with bedding plants. At the rear a gazebo supports hanging baskets.

Garden for Nature
The small wildlife garden situated to the rear of the Container Garden was featured at the 1995 Chelsea Flower Show. Designed by Hilde Wainstein and sponsored by Camas Building Materials with support from the RSPB, the garden uses hard materials from Bradstone.

The Eros Garden
Also featured at the 1995 Chelsea Flower Show and presented to the Society by its sponsor, the *Evening Standard*, was this garden by Julie Toll. Of special note are the living willow fence and whitebeams trained to form the arbour and gate arch.

The Garden for Disabled People
With generous sponsorship from the Horticultural Society of Messrs Coutts and Co, a new Garden for Disabled People was opened in May 1992. The design embodies ideas gained from its predecessor and has taken into account a wider range of disabilities. There is an ornamental pool at different levels, an impressive sculpture by Polly Ionides and a range of scented and tactile plants to bring pleasure to the senses.

The Garden for Disabled People incorporates features for people with a wide range of disabilities. Wildlife is encouraged at Wisley, which some species, like these mallards, fully appreciate

GLASSHOUSES

Opposite: In the Cool Section, the November display of *Dendranthema* is composed of charm and cascade chrysanthemums trained into a variety of pleasing shapes

The Glasshouses are situated between the Fruit Field, Model Gardens and maintenance buildings. They can also be reached by a path from the Portsmouth Field or Battleston Hill.

Remember that the Glasshouses close at 4.15 p.m., Monday to Saturday and 4.45 p.m. on Sundays.

Main Display House

The Main Display House is divided into three temperature controlled sections and the central porch, flanked by a pair of standard camellias, leads into the Intermediate Section.

The Intermediate Section is kept at a minimum of 50 F (10 C), which is suitable for temperate plants, and should provide plenty of inspiration for owners of conservatories. There are hibiscus, bougainvilleas, strelitzias, brugmansia with great hanging white trumpets, huge stag's horn ferns and arum lilies. Many other plants from countries a little warmer than Britain luxuriate in these conditions. Passion flowers, including the banana passion fruit *Passiflora antioquiensis*, strung with dark pink parachutes in late summer to autumn, are especially prolific and there is a corner devoted to ferns. Houseplants abound, including the familiar cyclamen, begonias, shrimp plants and poinsettias. There is also an informative selection of plants recommended for various temperatures in the home.

Ivy, *Lotus berthelotii* and cyclamen make an eye-catching container planting to enhance the fine plant of strelitzia in the Intermediate Section of the Main Display House

The Cool Section, to the right of the entrance, is maintained at a minimum temperature of 40 F (5 C), which allows a wide range of slightly tender climbers and shrubs to be grown. Among them are the parrot's bill, *Clianthus puniceus*, with claw-shaped pink flowers, the large South African heath, *Erica canaliculata, Abutilon megapotamicum*, with red and yellow

lantern flowers and bomareas, which resemble climbing alstroemerias. A major feature of this section is the seasonal shows of pot plants and annuals for forcing. In November, the display of *Dendranthema*, composed of charm and cascade chrysanthemums trained into standards, fans, pyramids and other artistic shapes is always a great attraction.

The Warm Section, at the other end of the Display House, is for plants requiring a minimum temperature of 60 F (16 C) and feels uncomfortably humid to humans. South American allamandas, with flamboyant yellow flowers, and anthuriums, with waxy, palette-shaped flower spathes, passion flowers and other exotica grow in profusion. Bromeliads, that intriguing family of plants to which the pineapple belongs, are represented by garish guzmanias and vriesias, with tillandsias perched on a tree. Pitcher plants, *Nepenthes* species, grow in various containers, some hanging. Look out for their intriguing insect-trapping pitchers. The presence of such striking foliage plants as *Ctenanthe, Calathea* and *Peperomia* may explain why these are rarely happy in the average living room, unless given sufficient humidity. Connected to this section by a short corridor is the Singapore Airlines Orchid Display House which was constructed and planted up during 1991 and opened in November of that year. Here the plants are on show in both

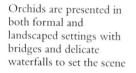

Orchids are presented in both formal and landscaped settings with bridges and delicate waterfalls to set the scene

formal and landscaped settings. Although the more spectacular species are in flower during winter and spring, many interesting and decorative forms are to be seen at other times. In the summer a collection of *Caladium* hybrids is displayed.

Additional Glasshouses

Two further glasshouses, accessible from the Intermediate Section of the display houses are used for trials and seasonal displays.

The Vinery, a small glasshouse at the far end of one of these accommodates a range of grape cultivars suitable for growing under glass, a mouth-watering sight before autumn harvest, even from the outside.

The remaining glasshouses, reserved for teaching, examinations, propagation and growing on, are not open.

The Orchid Display House is a warm retreat in January, where numerous exotic blooms, such as this *Odontoglossum* hybrid delight the senses

However, a stroll through the connecting corridors yields some fine examples of the pink *Bougainvillea* 'Miss Manila', numerous begonias, rubber plants, citrus plants, ferns and various flowering pot plants in season. Carnivorous plants are also prominent in the summer. Baskets hanging from the cross bars are adorned with the brilliant red flowers of *Columnea gloriosa* and *Aeschynanthus* spp.

A path on the easterly side of the Main Display House runs alongside the complex to a group of smaller glasshouses. One of these holds orchids being grown on for display and is not open to the public.

The Cacti and Succulents House is located between the main Glasshouse range and the Portsmouth Field. One year, a blackbird surprisingly selected a large cactus here in which to build its nest from which the young were fledged successfully.

In the borders and raised beds outside the glasshouses amaryllis, watsonias, nerines, crinums and other slightly tender bulbs make a colourful display in summer and autumn along with yuccas. Other areas are bedded out with various subtropical plants giving massed foliage displays.

The new double-span glasshouses, not open to the public, are a valuable addition to the research and propagation facilities of the Garden.

Before you leave the glasshouses, consider for a moment the very wide range of skills and expertise among the staff to enable them to deal with the demands of the great range of plants grown here. Also, their constant vigilance outwits pests through an active and successful control programme including biological methods.

Exit the main Glasshouse and with your back to the main entrance turn left where, round the corner, is the informative Plant Demonstration Area.

12

PLANT DEMONSTRATION AREA

At the top of the slope on the left over a hundred different sorts of hedging plant are on view, from formally clipped to informal and flowering hedges. All were planted in the same year, 1980, so that the rates of growth can be compared. These are interspersed with blocks of low-growing plants, illustrating the potential of ground cover in both sun and shade.

Back on the main path, after the Demonstration, is the entrance to the Fruit Field. If you have time there is much of interest. Beyond the Fruit Field is stage 3 of the Jubilee Arboretum (page 18).

Otherwise, go the Model Fruit Gardens, which are opposite (page 28).

FRUIT FIELD

The fruit collection has been called a living library of fruit. It is situated in a 6.5-ha (16-acre) field at the top of Weather Hill, beyond the Model Fruit Gardens and the Glasshouses. Half of it is taken up with apples, comprising over 670 cultivars, the majority of which were planted in the early 1950s. They are growing on M 7 and MM 106 semi-dwarf rootstocks (recommended for small early-fruiting trees). Since 1991 part of the collection has been replanted as spindle-bush trees grafted on the dwarfing rootstock M 26 and are divided into eating and cooking apples, arranged according to their season of ripening. There is also a block of virus-tested apples on the dwarfing M 26 rootstock.

In September the Fruit Field yields its apple harvest

One hundred and twenty of the leading cultivars of pear are grown on Quince A rootstock, again grouped by season. One hundred dessert plums and gages are grafted on the semi-dwarfing rootstock Pixy, which is generally considered the most satisfactory, and are trained as pyramids. Luckily, the Fruit Field suffered relatively lightly in the storm of October 1987, but a shelter belt has been planted to replace the Monterey pines at the western end. Quinces, medlars and nuts are also grown in the Fruit Field.

In the northeastern area of the Fruit Field, close to the entrance and linked to the Model Fruit Garden, a nursery and soft fruit area have recently been established. The latter holds collections of raspberries, blackcurrants, strawberries and hybrid berries, and a small vineyard containing both dessert and wine-making cultivars of outdoor grapes. In the nursery area, the propagation of rootstocks and fruit trees is demonstrated and the trees produced are used in the replanting programme for the orchard.

A variety of birds is attracted by the ripe fruit, and kestrels

Opposite: Cordon apples
in blossom in the Model
Fruit Garden. Training
fruit trees on cordons is a
suitable method for a
small garden

and sparrowhawks are attracted by the smaller birds. The blackbirds may strip the trees of fruit, helped by chaffinches and bramblings, fieldfares and redwings. In winter flocks of many species rest here.

Because of the Garden's susceptibility to spring frosts, the National Fruit Trials were moved from Wisley to Brogdale in Kent many years ago. However, the plantation remains a valuable reference collection, for new cultivars are constantly being added so that their qualities can be compared with those of the older established kinds, and a system for trialling fruits for the Award of Garden Merit was introduced in 1992.

14

MORE MODEL GARDENS

Model Fruit Gardens

The Model Fruit Gardens exhibit a breathtaking variety of fruit and there are many lessons here in how to obtain a good yield of hardy fruits from a small garden. Modern dwarfing rootstocks are used for apples and pears, and trees are trained as spindlebushes and in restricted forms as cordons, espaliers, fans and pyramids. Soft fruits – black, white and red currants, gooseberries and raspberries – are grown too, some as standards, but strawberries have been allocated a separate plot, where a system of soil rotation can be practised.

The westerly section contains a large collection of soft fruits and some examples of less familiar fruits, such as blueberries and jostaberries, as well as indoor grapes, apricots and peaches. The latter are protected with a polythene screen in winter against peach leaf curl. Figs and apples look quite content growing in large clay pots.

The Herb Garden

Immediately opposite the entrance to the Glasshouses is the much enjoyed Herb Garden, formally arranged with box hedges, urns and other containers. It contains a wide

assortment of culinary and medicinal herbs, mixed with aromatic plants. Tea and tisane plants, insect-repelling plants and economic plants are given special sections.

There is another chance to look at the Model Fruit Gardens before crossing the expanse of lawn to the rose catenary and the Bowes Lyon Pavilion.

OR, return to the walk in front of the Glasshouse, go back down the walk the way you came and turn left at the borders flanking the path to Weather Hill.

TO WEATHER HILL

Two broad borders flank the route from the Glasshouses to Weather Hill, each backed by a pyracantha hedge and standard trees of *Buddleja alternifolia* making cascades of scented lilac blossom in summer. The borders are devoted to hardy and half-hardy annuals, both traditional favourites and less common kinds, and present an enchanting display from late June to August.

Almost half-way along turn left in the opening and walk up the Rose Catenary to the Bowes Lyon Pavilion, or start from the bottom of the rose borders to enjoy the full effect.

15

WEATHER HILL

Weather Hill takes its name from the meteorological station which once stood at the top, before being moved to the Fruit Field. From the bottom of the hill, where there are two good specimens of the maidenhair tree, the living fossil *Ginkgo biloba*, the land sweeps up. The open grassy slopes are home to many noteworthy trees and shrubs, interspersed with flowering cherries and ornamental crabs. Near the foot of the hill on the right, *Buddleja alternifolia* forms a beautiful low tree. Close by, *Magnolia liliiflora* 'Nigra' opens large, deep purple chalice-shaped flowers in May. The Judas tree, *Cercis siliquastrum*, produces tufts of rosy red flowers direct from the wood before the heart-shaped leaves appear. In June, *Cornus kousa* is wreathed in a mass of white bracts, giving way to brilliant red foliage in October, when the leaves of the red bud maple, *Acer trautvetteri*, turn butter yellow. Look for a splendid Indian bean tree, *Catalpa bignonioides*.

On the left-hand side of the walk stands a majestic black walnut, *Juglans nigra*, and higher up, the twisted branches of *Robinia pseudoacacia* 'Tortuosa' make an interesting silhouette. In June the golden pineapple-scented flowers and silvery leaves of *Cytisus battandieri* are particularly striking, as are the yellow fronds of *Gleditsia triacanthos* 'Sunburst'.

Two shapely specimens of the uncommon *Phellodendron amurense* var. *sachalinense* can be found near by. Above these are the Kentucky coffee tree, *Gymnocladus dioica*, with handsome large, divided leaves, which turn from pink to green, and the

On Weather Hill in July the Rose Borders come into their own with large-flowered and cluster-flowered bush roses

Cornus kousa is a mass of white bracts in June. Later on, in October, its foliage becomes a brilliant red splash on Weather Hill

two columnar tulip trees, *Liriodendron tulipifera* 'Fastigiatum'.

Rose Borders and Catenary The roses in the two long borders are graded according to colour. Large-flowered bush roses and cluster-flowered bush roses, better known as hybrid teas and floribundas, are still the most popular roses in English gardens and Weather Hill is the place to see them growing in splendid isolation.

On the far side of each of the rose borders the reinstated Rose Catenary of oak posts and ropes support twin chains of a variety of climbing roses. In high summer the Catenary and the rose borders prove an irresistible attraction.

The Bowes Lyon Pavilion This light and elegant structure is the focal point at the top of the hill. The Pavilion was completed in 1964 to commemorate Sir David Bowes Lyon, President of the Society from 1953 to 1961, and brother of HM Queen Elizabeth the Queen Mother (herself a patron of the Society). Derrick Lees, FRIBA, presented this winning design. The simple teak canopy of linked octagonal roofs on slender posts was designed according to a system of geometric proportion reflecting the columnar theme of the area dominated by two magnificent Dawyck beeches, *Fagus sylvatica* 'Dawyck'.

Slightly beyond the Pavilion, the well-named golden rain tree or pride of India, *Koelreuteria paniculata*, bears deep yellow flowers in summer. In the shrub border grow a number of old roses, underplanted with pulmonarias.

Having explored Weather Hill, standing in front of the Pavilion and with your back to it, walk to the left. Ahead are the Alpine Houses on the left, the Model Vegetable Garden on the right and the Monocot Borders in between.

ALPINE HOUSES

Two houses completed in 1984 replaced the original alpine house of 1926 and the surroundings have been totally redeveloped. Remember that the Alpine Houses close at 4.15 p.m. during the winter months.

The site faces north and is divided into three levels by dry-stone walls, constructed of different materials – Purbeck stone at the top and middle, Sussex sandstone at the bottom. The crevices in the walls accommodate a wealth of plants, from lewisias, convolvulus, zauschnerias and ferns higher up, to the shade-loving *Ramonda myconi*, with lavender-blue, saucer-shaped blooms and its paler-flowered relative, *Haberlea rhodopensis*, in the lowest and darkest spots.

Alpine Display House This traditional wooden alpine display house on the top terrace is used for alpines grown in pots. These are plunged into sand on the benches to keep

In February the Wooden Alpine House is full of warmth and colour. These diminutive alpines, grown in pots which are plunged into sand, can only delight in the winter months

watering to a minimum and are changed regularly to reflect the range of alpines in flower. New or reintroduced species collected from mountains all over the world are represented, together with early-flowering plants which can be grown to perfection when sheltered from winter weather. *Crocus sieberi* and the delightful cultivars of *C. chrysanthus* make their debut at the beginning of the year, to be joined by tender cyclamen like *C. pseudibericum, C. persicum* and the rare *C. trochopteranthum, Scilla tubergeniana (S. mischtschenkoana),* the star-like *Ipheion* 'Wisley Blue' and the diminutive white or pink buttercup, *Ranunculus calandrinioides.* To grow many of these plants to perfection, the Roy Elliott Alpine Supply House was donated to the Society in 1991 by the Alpine Garden Society and the family of the late Roy Elliott, an alpine enthusiast who served on the RHS Council.

Against the Alpine Display House is a south-facing rock bank of tufa, a very porous limestone, in which many fascinating plants flourish. Between this house and Weather Hill are two raised beds, one housing lime-tolerant plants, the other lime haters.

The Aluminium Alpine House The house was re-built during 1995–6 with generous financial assistance from the East Surrey Group of the Alpine Garden Society, Hendry Bequest Fund. A simulated dry gully runs between miniature cliffs up to 1.5 m (5 ft) high. The cliffs demonstrate several rock types and provide niches for difficult-to-please alpines. The watering system is computer-controlled with irrigation lines terminating in over 100 bubble points which trickle water gently to the root systems. The irrigation system is hidden beneath broken stones and the very gritty soil behind the rockwork. Two large fans circulate air, assisted by louvred vents along the side walls and large ridge vents running the length of the house. Outside, the theme continues, demonstrating various rock types and aspects and the alpines that grow well in these situations.

Hypertufa sinks and stone troughs on the lower terrace are ideal for small slow-growing alpines, such as sempervivums, sedums, saxifrages, silenes, phlox, campanulas and androsaces, which nestle between pieces of rock and slate and maintain a succession of bloom throughout the year. One minute trough is devoted entirely to silver saxifrages. More vigorous plants fill the gaps in the paving, which is a creamy buff colour to heighten the impression of light, while ferns,

hellebores and purple-black leaved ophiopogons grace the border below the lowest wall.

From this ridge there are 'secret' views of the Rock Garden. For the moment, resist the urge to plunge over the edge; rather, finish looking at this valuable area of the Garden.

MODEL VEGETABLE GARDEN

Go through the little gate, latching it behind you, and you will no doubt be welcomed by a territorial robin or two.

About 50 different vegetables, over 400 cultivars, are grown here each season, including award-winners from RHS trials whenever possible. Less common ones, such as salsify and chicory, are grown in a special border displaying a wide range of interesting crops.

The Model Vegetable Garden features many aspects of vegetable production including an average allotment-sized plot which is cropped to provide a family's annual needs. Good ideas to use in a limited space are always part of the presentation, and a patio garden demonstrates the use of tubs and troughs for vegetable growing.

Smaller plots demonstrate some of the principles of so-called organic gardening, and narrow beds 1.2m (4ft) wide are featured as a means of maximising site use, and for convenient working with reduced soil compaction.

Small areas are devoted to growing exhibition vegetables, and perennial vegetables such as asparagus, rhubarb, and globe artichokes, whilst the use of raised beds, containing highly fertile soil, provides an effective means of intensive vegetable growing. Tender subjects like melons and tomatoes, as well as early crops, are grown under greenhouse, frame, cloche and fleece protection – often in conjunction with mulches and novel irrigation methods, to minimise weeding and watering.

All waste from the Model Vegetable Garden is recycled, using the four compost bins on site. Information boards around this garden describe many of the

Harvest time approaches in the Model Vegetable Garden, where more than 50 vegetables and over 400 cultivars are grown each season

activities carried out, including crop-rotation. A list of cultivars grown, and where to buy them, can be obtained from the
Reception in the Laboratory building.

Leave the Model Vegetable Garden at the upper end (the
direction of the Bowes Lyon Pavilion), turn right and walk
back towards the Rock Garden between the Monocot Borders.

Ornamental cabbages
'Benihato' in the Model
Vegetable Garden add
colour and interest

THE MONOCOT BORDERS

The Monocot Borders, between the Model Vegetable Garden
and Alpine Houses, concentrate on one of the two great classes
of flowering plants – the monocotyledons. Plants such as *Agapanthus, Alstroemeria, Crocosmia, Hemerocallis, Iris, Kniphofia,
Lilium, Liriope, Phormium tenax, Sisyrinchium, Tradescantia,
Tricyrtis* and *Yucca,* combined with ornamental grasses, make a
rich spectacle in summer and autumn. The Monocot Borders
are a perfect approach path to the Rock Garden straight ahead.

ROCK GARDEN

The first sight of the Rock Garden at Wisley is never forgotten by most visitors. Numerous little paths lead down and around rocky outcroppings and small pools that are linked by streams and cascades, the water eventually flowing into the Long Ponds at the bottom. Towards the western end of the Rock Garden is the Grotto, one of the original features. At the

bottom here is the rustic bridge over the Long Ponds draped with *Wisteria floribunda* f. *macrobotrys*, whose beautiful lilac-blue and purple tassels reach down to the water in May, as they have done for almost a century. Explore the garden slowly moving in the direction of the Laboratory building.

Here the Long Ponds in the Rock Garden are cleared by trainee gardeners, part of a never-ending programme of improvement and renewal throughout the year

The Rock Garden was the first major project at Wisley, built by James Pulham & Son, specialists in large-scale rock gardens, to designs by the landscape architect, Edward White. A light railway was constructed to transport the stone into the garden. It is believed that the original positions of the sandstone were noted as it was being quarried and an attempt was made to duplicate this positioning at Wisley, hence the natural looking appearance of this garden. The Rock Garden tends to slip gently downhill, owing to the light sandy soil and underground springs, and requires constant renovation. This gave the opportunity for restoration. In the 1980s the southern section was largely reconstructed to the original design. Wealdon sandstone, quarried near East Grinstead, has been used in the past, and most recently sandstone from the Soil Hill Quarry near Halifax, Yorkshire has been found to be the closest possible match to the original Ashdown sandstone.

Opposite: A tranquil late autumn scene in the north-facing Rock Garden, where both shade-lovers and sun-seekers are happily accommodated

The steep slope faces north and suits many plants which prefer a cool shady spot, as the large and prosperous ramondas in the vertical cervices prove. There is ample room, too, on the more exposed outcrops for sun-loving plants. In April and May, the Rock Garden becomes a treasure trove of gentians,

daphnes, dianthus, pulsatillas, jeffersonias, phlox, gypsophila, hepatica, potentillas, primulas, saxifrages, and countless other alpines whose exquisite flowers repay close inspection.

Although spring is the main season, it is certainly not the only time to visit the Rock Garden. Snowdrops, crocuses, cyclamen, miniature irises and the scented, creamy-white *Daphne blagayana* begin the year and *Rhododendron* × *praecox*, near the top, lives up to its name with February flowers of rosy purple. Himalayan gentians sport their blue trumpets in autumn and *Polygonum vacciniifolium* retains its tiny pink flowers through the frosts, while small evergreen shrubs like *Skimmia japonica* ssp. *reevesiana* and *Sarcococca hookeriana* var. *digyna* contribute colourful berries and foliage in winter. Numerous dwarf conifers provide a permanent structure, among them the low drooping mound of *Tsuga canadensis* 'Pendula', near the main steps, and many small forms of *Chamaecyparis obtusa*, their flattened sprays of foliage giving them a three-dimensional quality.

Rhododendron 'Temple Belle' presides from a high point, with trusses of gorgeous, soft pink bells in April and roots straddling a large rock in bonsai fashion.

At the west end of the Rock Garden, snowdrops, hellebores, ground-covering pulmonarias and creamy-flowered comfrey, *Symphytum grandiflorum*, grow in an attractive tangle.

By the water, no one could miss the huge paddle-shaped leaves of the skunk cabbage, *Lysichiton americanum*, with its bold yellow flower spathes in March and April, or the grandiose umbrella plant, *Darmera peltata*, whose lustrous foliage turns red in autumn. Two British natives, the lemon-yellow globe flower, *Trollius europaeus*, and the marsh marigold or king cup, *Caltha palustris*, are happily established on the banks, where *Leucojum aestivum* 'Gravetye Giant', an improved form of the summer snowflake, also flowers – despite its name – in spring. Primulas of all kinds, astilbes, *Iris sibirica* and sumptuous *I. ensata (I. kaempferi)* cultivars (the latter a feature in the days of G F Wilson) continue the display, together with arum lilies, hostas, ferns, lady's mantle, *Alchemilla mollis*, and, at the far end a vast *Gunnera manicata*, big enough to shelter under. These broad ditches between the Rock Garden and the Wild Garden are a haven for ducks and tadpoles and a quantity of moisture-loving plants.

ALPINE MEADOW

The dramatic Rock Garden merges gradually into the gentler Alpine Meadow, a grassy slope facing the Wild Garden and dotted with outcrops of rock at the upper west end. In the meadow look for two examples of *Acer palmatum* 'Dissectum Atropurpureum'. These hardy Japanese maples make neat hummocks of delicately cut, deep red leaves, becoming bronze and yellow in autumn.

During late March and early April, the grass is transformed into a sheet of sulphur-yellow from thousands of naturalised hoop-petticoat daffodils, *Narcissus bulbocodium*. Further up the slope of the Alpine Meadow *Narcissus triandrus* succeeds the main display and joins company with *Anemone nemorosa* – blue wood anemones, pink and white dog's tooth violets, *Erythronium denscanis*, and drifts of *Fritillaria meleagris*, the snake's-head fritillary, all of which enjoy shade from the overhanging trees. Later, in autumn, the purple flowers of *Crocus nudiflorus* appear and are closely followed by *Crocus kotschyanus* with flowers of a lighter mauve or lilac. *Crocus speciosus* may also be found in small numbers at this time of year.

Walk straight on in the direction of the Laboratory building and you soon come to a water feature. Follow the path beside the water, also admiring the stately shapes of the trees on Conifer Lawn on the left.

One of the annual spectacles of Wisley: naturalised hoop-petticoat daffodils, *Narcissus bulbocodium*, in the Alpine Meadow

THOMPSON MEMORIAL WATER FEATURE AND BOWLES' CORNER

The water feature, named after a local businessman, was built in 1992-3. It is a series of pools and beds at the eastern end of the Alpine Meadow to the rear of Weather Hill Cottage. Follow the path beside the stream up the hill to Bowles' Corner, a somewhat hidden spot, where you will find a bench by the head of the stream and a wonderful view. This area is dedicated to the great gardener, E A Bowles, who enjoyed a long association with the Society, from his election to Council in 1908 until his death in 1954, and conveyed his love of gardening to a wide audience through his entertaining trilogy of books, *My Garden in Spring, Summer* and *Autumn and Winter.*

The water feature near Bowles' Corner, added to the Garden in 1992-3

Follow the water feature back up the hill around Weather Hill Cottage to examine the gardens around the cottage and at Bowles' Corner.

Bowles had a penchant for what he called 'demented plants – departing from normal habit or appearance' and some of these are included in Bowles' Corner. A hawthorn and a hazel, each with extraordinary corkscrew branches, demand a second look, as do familiar plants like *Symphoricarpos orbiculatus* and London Pride, *Saxifraga* × *urbium*, in their variegated versions.

In winter, *Garrya elliptica* is draped with long suede-grey catkins and later the donkey's ear snowdrop, *Galanthus nivalis* 'Scharlockii' appears, with long spathes or 'ears' projecting above the flowers. Crocuses and colchicums reflect another of Bowles' special interests, with *Crocus sieberi* 'Bowles' White' and *Colchicum bowlesianum* (correctly *C. bivonae*) named after him. Several other plants preserve his memory in the same way; two for instance are *Malus* 'Bowles' Hybrid' and the stately ornamental rhubarb, *Rheum palmatum* 'Bowles' Red'. Bowles' famous two-pronged dividing fork is on display.

Round the corner of the house the fibrous trunk of a Chusan palm, *Trachycarpus fortunei*, strikes an exotic note, one of several in this part of the garden. Further on are terraced banks, packed with dwarf rhododendrons and other peat-loving plants – cassiopes, *Pieris japonica*, primulas, gentians, cyclamen, hostas, meconopsis and ferns.

Go back down the path to the front of the original home of G F Wilson, 'Oakwood', now called Weather Hill Cottage, which lies set back from the path and is a very early example of a prefabricated house. To the left of its gate, a small collection of daphnes has been assembled.

This is another opportunity to take a closer look at the Summer Garden, ahead (page 10).

For a more extensive walk, return to the front of the Laboratory building and carry on with the walk below.

Semi-Woodland Walk

19

LABORATORY BUILDING

From the Main Entrance, walk in front of the Laboratory building where the beautiful *Carpenteria californica* grows. This shrubby evergreen produces pure white flowers with golden-yellow anthers in June and July.

To the left of the front door stands the chaste tree, *Vitex agnus-castus* f. *latifolia*, hung with fragrant blue panicles in September and October. Further down, *Parthenocissus henryana* and *Actinidia kolomikta* display their striking foliage and *Azara serrata* contributes yellow powder puffs in early summer. By the archway, *Camellia japonica* 'Princess Charlotte' has been known to open its elegant mixture of pink and white blooms in

January, when *Viburnum foetens* makes its presence felt with white, heavily perfumed flowers.

Perennials and small shrubs, many of them the envy of gardeners in colder districts, fill the borders around the Laboratory building and supply a wealth of colour in summer and autumn. Salvias and diascias mingle with *Callistemon* (bottle brush), *Hedychium* (hardy ginger), as well as the South African *Agapanthus* and *Watsonia*. Two curiosities are *Lobelia tupa*, which has spikes of claw-like, red-brown flowers, and *Cuphea cyanea*, with little red and yellow cigars. In the autumn, the belladonna lily, *Amaryllis belladonna*, unfolds its pink trumpets,

along with the more slender *Nerine bowdenii*. In autumn, *Colquhounia coccinea* gives a fine display of orange-red tubular flowers.

In the lawn near the front door, a pool has been filled in and is now used for displays of carpet bedding, which are renewed with a different design each year.

In front of the Laboratory building views have been opened up by the improved access for wheelchairs. The main features are a series of flat terraces starting from a round paved area, with a curved wall seat and central birdbath, whose column is a relic of the original Waterloo Bridge. The large tree dominating the terraces is *Hippophae rhamnoides* subsp. *yunnanensis*, a Chinese form of our native sea buckthorn. It is one of Wisley's 'champion trees', which means it is recorded as the largest example growing in Britain.

Garden staff take great care in planting out carpet bedding in front of the Laboratory building. Each year a new design is drawn up, with the aim of preserving this fine tradition

CANAL AND LOGGIA

The Laboratory building overlooks a formal stretch of water known as the 'Canal'. Strewn with an extensive collection of water lilies, it is flanked by panels of grass and ends in an open-ended pavilion (the Loggia). This area was the site of the old glasshouses, redeveloped in the early 1970s to designs by the landscape architects, Lanning Roper and Sir Geoffrey Jellicoe.

A collection of water lilies floats lanquidly on the surface of the Canal

Walk along the wide path on the right-hand side of the Canal. The broad mixed border here faces south, and is composed mainly of summer-flowering shrubs and perennials. The beds are edged with English lavender (*Lavandula angustifolia*) and the seats are backed by English roses, with their summer-long display of sumptuous blooms. A large specimen of *Parrotia persica* makes an effective backdrop, particularly in autumn with its beautifully tinted foliage. Clematis are allowed to scramble over the spreading junipers.

At the end of the Canal, walk on to the Loggia, cleverly constructed to give the impression of being a bridge. This, less prosaically, was the potting shed when glasshouses stood where the Canal is now sited. A visitor told staff of taking exams in this structure many years ago. From the Loggia is perhaps the most famous view at Wisley and one of the most beautiful – that of the Laboratory building in its luxuriant setting. Look for the large golden orfe in the Canal.

Near the steps by the Loggia are cut-leaved cultivars of the popular Japanese maple, *Acer palmatum* Dissectum group with red, orange and yellow Autumn colour.

With your back to the Laboratory building walk into the Formal Garden, then the Walled Garden beyond.

20

FORMAL GARDEN

Beyond the Loggia lies the Formal Garden, then the Walled Garden, bisected by a path between clipped yew hedges. Both are on a scale which the ordinary gardener can appreciate.

The first is laid out as a formal parterre and used for a variety of spring and summer bedding schemes, creating a rainbow of colour visible from the Laboratory building. In this central bed a tradition of formal planting is maintained utilising thousands of plants. The south-facing wall, on the right, supports roses, *Passiflora, Ceanothus* 'Delight', *Clematis armandii* and *Cytisus battandieri*. At their feet are pomegranates and white-flowered *Carpenteria californica*, underplanted with dwarf bearded iris, diascias, *Nerine bowdenii* and *Amaryllis* – sun-lovers all. Plants enjoying cooler shaded conditions adorn the north-facing border. Among them are *Holboella, Lapageria, Hydrangea petiolaris*, roses and *Pyracantha*. The shrub layer includes aralias and daphnes, with *Hamamelis* × *intermedia* 'Pallida' and *Stachyurus chinensis* 'Magpie', underplanted with *Sarcoccoca*, Japanese anemones, hellebores and *Polystichum* ferns.

In the Formal Garden, a diversity of tulips give pattern and colour to the spring bedding

WALLED GARDEN

December mists envelop the yew hedges that divide the Formal and Walled Gardens

An archway draped with roses leads to the second, more intimate, Walled Garden. The beds are arranged round a central fountain and planted with old and modern shrub roses, whose soft colours are enhanced by grey and silver foliage plants, blending with phlox, irises, columbines, scabious, lilies, day lilies, agapanthus and Japanese anemones to give a cottage-garden atmosphere. The strange *Lobelia tupa* strikes a more unexpected note in autumn. The Chinese gooseberry, *Actinidia chinensis*, the exuberant evergreen *Holboellia latifolia*, the boldly variegated *Hedera canariensis* 'Variegata' and *H. colchica* 'Sulphur Heart' and the extremely narrow-leaved *H.* 'Bill Archer', roses and clematis clamber over the walls, with *Piptanthus laburnifolius* beneath and *Robinia pseudoacacia* 'Frisia' near by.

At the far end of the Walled Garden, the double gates offer a tantalising glimpse of the Alpine Meadow and the Wild Garden. The gates commemorate Ken Aslet, a member of the Wisley staff from 1949 to 1975 and for many years Superintendent of the Rock Garden.

The gate in the north wall, framing a magnificent view of Seven Acres, is dedicated to Frank Knight, Director of Wisley from 1955 to 1969. Opposite this is a third gate, presented in memory of W D Cartwright, who worked at Wisley for 44 years.

Just outside this gate on the right are some specimens of *Magnolia grandiflora*. Magnolias have been in this area since 1915. The southerly side of the wall provides a support for wisteria. The fragrant, pale-orange flowers of *Trachelospermum asiaticum* in July and August recall miniature gardenias and *Abeliophyllum distichum* responds to summer baking by blossoming in January. Clematis are represented by the uncommon winter-flowering *C. napaulensis, C. rehderiana*, producing soft primrose-yellow blooms in autumn, and a tangle of *C. cirrhosa* var. *balearica*, strung with tiny, cream, spotted bells from September to March. At their feet is a border of irises, tulip species, colchicums and tender watsonias. As part of the Conifer Lawn re-development new beds have been made for plants enjoying a hot dry position, including a collection of ceanothus. Straight ahead, on the other side of the path, is the Wild Garden.

WILD GARDEN

The Wild Garden is the most historic part of Wisley and, although much altered since the time of G F Wilson, it has kept entirely to the spirit of his original woodland garden. Wilson recorded almost 22,000 separate plantings in 'Oakwood', from 1878 until his death in 1902.

The soil is peaty and more moisture-retentive than elsewhere in the Garden, which was ideal for woodland plants until storms depleted the tree canopy. Other trees now compete in stature with the oaks, particularly the umbrella pine, *Sciadopitys verticillata*, with leaves arranged like umbrella spokes, and *Chamaecyparis pisifera* 'Squarrosa', both of which were planted some 80 years ago, and the fast-growing dawn redwood, *Metasequoia glyptostroboides*, which was raised from the first introduction of seed in 1948.

The taller trees and several more cypresses are grouped in the Seven Acres end of the Wild Garden, where *Eucryphia* × *nymansensis* 'Nymansay', on a mound overlooking the Alpine

Foxgloves and rhododendrons in the Wild Garden, the most historic part of Wisley, which maintains the spirit of G F Wilson's original woodland garden

Meadow, is a fine sight in August, carrying white yellow-anthered flowers among shining evergreen leaves. Two of a somewhat neglected genus, *Stewartia pseudocamellia* and *S. serrata*, revel in the shade, producing white cup-shaped summer blooms, and the beautiful snowbell, *Styrax japonica*, is hung with pure white flowers in June. These keep company with the white-bracted *Cornus kousa*, *Fothergilla monticola*,

notable for its bottle-brush flowers and autumn colour, the sweet pepper bush, *Clethra alnifolia*, bearing long fragrant racemes, *Oxydendrum arboreum* and a small paperbark maple, *Acer griseum*.

As in natural woodland, the lower-growing trees and shrubs make up the next layer of vegetation. They include numerous *Camellia japonica* cultivars, showing a wide range of colours and flower forms, magnolias of many sorts, starting with *Magnolia × soulangeana* and *M. kobus* in April and finishing in late summer with the scented creamy white blooms of *M. virginiana*, and some massive old *Rhododendron ponticum* hybrids. Close relatives of rhododendrons are the *Enkianthus* species and the splendid *Pieris japonica*, all with drooping urn-shaped flowers in spring, and the kalmias, with

Springtime drifts of *Narcissus cyclamineus* under the trees in the Wild Garden

pink cup-shaped blooms in summer. *Enkianthus* develop intense foliage colour in autumn, while the heart-shaped leaves of *Disanthus cercidifolius* turn a stunning claret red, followed by undistinguished maroon flowers in November. Members of the witch hazel family also like an acid soil and festoon themselves with fragrant primrose-yellow blossoms early in the year.

The floor of the woodland is home to an immense variety of plants, which also perform the important service of checking weeds – from shrubby carpeters, such as vacciniums and gaultherias, to hostas, pulmonarias, epimediums and the intriguing mouse plant, *Arisarum proboscideum*, whose long-tailed flowers lurk amid spear-shaped leaves. Retired and former staff members when visiting have recounted how some of the now magnificent trees were taken as seedlings from nearby Wisley Common.

At dawn one morning, a member of staff came upon a mother mink shepherding six cubs and encouraging a straggler from one watery spot to another in the Wild Garden. These predators are attracted by the birds' nests, and they too are part of nature's cycle.

In spring, drifts of *Narcissus cyclamineus* and other daffodils like *N.* 'W P Milner', wood anemones, both *Anemone nemorosa* and *A. apennina*, and hellebores are punctuated with more unusual plants. Among these may be American dog's tooth violets, *Erythronium americanum*, and *E. revolutum*, the wake robin, *Trillium grandiflorum*, in pure white and the dark maroon *Trillium sessile* 'Rubrum'.

The parade of primulas commences before winter is over with the cheerful pink and red flowers of *P. vulgaris* subsp. *sibthorpii*, continues in early summer with the vivid candelabra primulas and closes with the large citron-yellow blooms of *P. florindae*.

Other plants enjoying woodland garden conditions are the yellow foxglove, *Digitalis lutea*, the willow gentian, *Gentiana asclepiadea*, astilbes, cultivars of *Iris sibirica* and the prolific white bellflower, *Campanula latifolia* f. *alba*. Also of interest is *Lobelia* 'Queen Victoria' and cultivars of both *Ligularia* and *Inula*.

Later on lilies grace the scene, especially the orange *Lilium superbum* and the panther lily, *L. pardalinum*. Campions and foxgloves emphasise the wildness of the garden, as does the lovely white form of the rosebay willow herb, *Epilobium angustifolium*, that common weed of wasteland. The white form is, however, less invasive.

After the storms a large amount of redesigning and restoration has been necessary and beds have been cleared and planted in rotation. The long-term objective is to restock the area with hostas, primulas, trilliums and the many other woodlanders that find the high water table and fertile soil so conducive to their growth. The 1988 replanting of the western boundary is making rapid progress and a bamboo walk has been introduced on the exposed southwest flank to filter the wind. A new network of paths and an irrigation system are also being installed.

22

SEVEN ACRES

Seven Acres is an oblong piece of land of approximately that size (2.5ha), bounded by the Wild Garden, the River Wey, the Pinetum and the Restaurant. Originally rough pasture, it was regarded as useless for cultivation until, in the 1920s, an iron pan was discovered just below the surface and broken up so that plant roots could reach the water. This operation has allowed successful cultivation of plants ever since, despite its sandy soil.

Ilex × *altaclerensis* 'Camelliifolia', with smooth camellia-like foliage as the name implies, the bright yellow-leaved *Quercus rubra* 'Aurea', *Acer griseum*, with its distinctive peeling bark, and the handsome eastern relative of the elm, *Zelkova serrata*, supply an interesting background. In this area is an example of the handkerchief tree, *Davidia involucrata*, planted on his retirement by Chris Brickell, the Society's first Director General, and also Director of Wisley from 1969 to 1985.

The Lake in Seven Acres. December's ice, frost and mist create an evocative image

The Lake

At the Wild Garden end of Seven Acres, facing the Restaurant, the Lake is ahead on the left. This man-made pool is a major water feature here where the conical outlines of three dawn redwoods, *Metasequoia glyptostroboides*, are reflected in its waters above a fringe of gunneras and several small willows. The Lake has a mood for all seasons, particularly in summer when the water lilies are out and again in autumn when the red-woods are burnished pink and old gold.

Around the Lake, flowering quinces, cherries and crabs, magnolias, philadelphus or mock oranges and fuchsias ensure a succession of bloom and, in May, the weeping willow-leaved pear, *Pyrus salicifolia* 'Pendula', is at its silvery best. The Chinese fringe tree, *Chionanthus retusus*, which has been likened to a 'dome of soft, fleecy snow', produces more of a flurry at Wisley, which perhaps explains why it is seldom seen in British gardens. A little later, the fragrant flowers of the pendent white lime, *Tilia* 'Petiolaris', prove irresistible to bees, which then fall to the ground in a narcotic haze and sometimes never recover.

The lake is a great attraction for birdlife. Occasionally a kingfisher may use the rescue pole as a perch from which to

A crocus bank in Seven Acres

fish. At least two pairs of these elusive birds are known to nest along the River-side Walk.

Autumn brings the gorgeous crimson foliage of the sweet gum, *Liquidambar styraciflua*, complemented by the scarlet, orange and yellow of the ground-sweeping tupelo, *Nyssa sylvatica*, both of them relishing the slightly marshy conditions. At the western end of Seven Acres, interest centres around Chinese and Japanese witch hazels at the turn of the year. *Hamamelis mollis* and *H. japonica* 'Superba' display yellow, scented spider-like flowers on leafless stems from December onwards when the winter sweet, *Chimonanthus praecox*, and the shrubby honeysuckle, *Lonicera × purpusii* contribute their heady fragrance. As the

The Round Pond in January. In summer it is easy to miss because it is almost hidden by foliage

season comes to a close, white berries of *Sorbus hupehensis* may be seen, standing out in contrast with the red foliage, whilst the shrub borders close by glisten with fruits, and the leaves of *Parrotia persica* turn rich gold and crimson.

In the Lake is a small island, where healthy clumps of *Gunnera manicata*, and the royal fern, *Osmunda regalis*, line the water's edge beneath a swamp cypress, *Taxodium distichum*. Look carefully and you will see its 'knees', knobbly aerial roots through which the tree takes in oxygen to compensate for the waterlogged conditions in which it grows. Seven Acres is in a frost pocket and the Lake sometimes freezes in winter. When the mallards find themselves skating across the ice, the head mallard may lead a long and hopeful procession to other watery places in the Garden.

The Round Pond

The Round Pond sits beside the Lake to the right (east), when the visitor faces the Restaurant. It is easy to miss because of the foliage surrounding it. The Pond started life in Wisley's early developments as a source of gravel for garden paths and has remained as a water feature, shunning the adverse effects of drought ever since.

On the little island stands a deep green Japanese umbrella pine, *Sciadopitys verticillata*.

The superb smoke bush, *Cotinus coggygria*, is enveloped in a cloud of pinkish plumes in summer, followed by flaming autumn leaves, and a fine fastigiate English oak towers above.

Around the base of the silver maple, *Acer saccharinum*, on the opposite bank, the parasitic *Lathraea clandestina* (which grows on the roots of trees) resembles livid purple cushions early in the year. A strong perfume emanates from the otherwise discreet, winter-flowering honeysuckle, *Lonicera standishii*. The shrub beds near the Round Pond are liberally planted with viburnums and philadelphus, as well as rubus, escallonias, deutzias, weigelas and berberis. *Wisteria venusta*, a climber which is grown here as a specimen shrub and has the largest individual flowers of all the wisterias, and the charming *Aesculus parviflora*, a bushy plant with white horse-chestnut blossom borne most profusely in July and August are of particular interest. *Prunus serrulata* 'Shirotae' steals the show in April, when the spreading branches carry clusters of pendent, snow-white fragrant flowers. In near by beds, daffodils give way to peonies, bergenias, red hot pokers and Michaelmas daisies. Day lilies, *Hemerocallis* cultivars, are well represented, demonstrating their fine qualities.

A group of trees to the south of the Round Pond includes *Quercus cerris* 'Variegata', the rare variegated Turkey oak (there is another in the Jubilee Arboretum), and the equally, but more deservedly rare *Cladrastis wilsonii*, which has never yet flowered,

and *Magnolia acuminata*, known as the cucumber tree for its short, green, young fruits. The white bark of *Betula* 'Silver Shadow' is noticeable, near a bush of *Hydrangea petiolaris*, normally seen as a climber but here grown as a most effective, low, spreading shrub, and a variegated form of the tulip tree, *Liriodendron tulipiferum* 'Aureomarginatum'.

Near here Robin Herbert planted a cultivar of the common beech, *Fagus sylvatica* 'Dawyck Gold' to mark his decade as President of the RHS (1984-94).

Continue your sweep around this end of the Garden to the Pinetum and the Riverside Walk (page 56), and Howard's Field and the Heather Garden (page 57). **OR**, if you wish to save those walks for another day, make your return journey via the front of the Restaurant (page 57).

Autumn visitors come to admire the leaves, feed the birds and absorb the tranquillity

PINETUM

A fine specimen of *Picea breweriana* in the Pinetum on a September day. Shrubs and trees are being planted here to give seasonal colour.

North-west of the Restaurant is the River Wey and the pumping station for the Garden. Follow the path beside the pumping station and under the fenced Public Right of Way. This ancient right of way enjoyed by joggers and walkers has been preserved, even though it cuts through the Pinetum.

Visitors in wheelchairs can only enter and leave this section by the unmade-up path under the Public Right of Way. The only other way out is over a stepped bridge.

As elsewhere in the Garden, out of the upheaval created by the storms has come the opportunity for major redevelopment in the Pinetum. Shrubs and trees chosen for autumn and spring colour, such as Japanese maples, witch hazels and flowering dogwoods, are being integrated with the existing conifers on the south side of the Public Right of Way.

Stroll through the Pinetum and on to Howard's Field, **OR**, take the alternative, tranquil riverside path with views of the River Wey. This route passes through a natural and undeveloped area frequented by many birds and other wildlife. If you are lucky, you may glimpse one of our resident kingfishers. Look out, too, for grey wagtails and other waterside birds, then continue to the Heather Garden in Howard's Field.

56

HOWARD'S FIELD AND THE HEATHER GARDEN

In Howard's Field a new heather garden has been established. The sight of the huge cushion-like beds of heather in luxuriant hues is a reward for visitors who travel to this northern tip of Wisley Garden. An irrigation system, with copious quantities of manure and leafmould dug in during the early stages of development, help in an area of otherwise pure sand. The heather beds, divided by meandering paths, have been placed for visual impact in groups of about 30 plants per cultivar. There are over 1,000 species, and cultivars of *Erica, Calluna* and *Daboecia* form part of the National Collection. A refreshing change from the usual accompaniment of dwarf conifers are andromedas, gaultherias and *Ozothamnus*. A major collection of birches is in the vicinity. Return along the side of the Garden furthest away from the river, back into the Pinetum.

Below: Each cushion-like bed in the Heather Garden contains about 30 plants per cultivar.

PINETUM CONTINUES TO RESTAURANT

Walking back through the collection of conifers, there are still many fine old specimens, in spite of being devastated in the 1990 storm. Deer sometimes swim the River Wey to reach this part of the Garden. Early one morning a member of staff saw a week-old fawn curled up on the soft carpet of needles under a conifer tree. Conifers have obvious attractions for many birds too, from goldcrest and finches to the green woodpecker, whose laughing call or 'yaffle' you may hear in the mature and impressive trees.

Return to the Restaurant area via the vine-covered bridge over the Public Right of Way and continue this pleasant stroll through the rest of the Pinetum, where narcissus may be spotted in early spring.

Below: Distinctive cones of *Pinus × holfordiana*, a very ornamental tree in the Pinetum

RESTAURANT TO
LABORATORY BUILDING

The Terrace Restaurant on a sunny October day. Aberconway House, on the right, is the hostel for trainee gardeners. Named after Lord Aberconway, a former President of the RHS, it was opened in 1954 by HM Queen Elizabeth, the Queen Mother

At the Restaurant end of Seven Acres is an English oak planted by HRH The Prince of Wales in 1993, and a tulip tree, *Liriodendron tulipifera*, planted by HM the Queen Mother in 1954, when she opened the Restaurant and the Students' Hostel, Aberconway House. The latter is named for the 2nd Lord Aberconway, President of the RHS for 22 years (1931-53).

The bed alongside Aberconway House is planted with a range of sun-loving plants in hot colours, including gazanias, Pacific Coast irises, *Crocosmia*, half-hardy perennial *Salvia*. Various climbing shrubs are trained against the wall.

The path leading from the Restaurant back to the Laboratory building passes two beds devoted to ornamental grasses and sedges of interest throughout the year. The white, cream or silvery pink plumes of pampas grass, *Cortaderia selloana*, are unmistakable towering above the clumps of *Miscanthus sinensis*, some with arching sprays of flowers. Further contrasts of shape and colour, with purples, blues and reds, are provided by other grasses, fescues and other plants.

In front of the Laboratory building admire again the Canal and Loggia in their perfect setting within this grand garden.

THE SEASONS AT WISLEY: WHEN TO VISIT – WHAT TO SEE

Here is a sampling of a few of the seasonal highlights, among very many. Areas are mentioned as well as some specific plants. As every gardener knows, flowering times may vary slightly. There are fine displays in the Glasshouses throughout the year, including the more tranquil winter months (a good place to warm up before continuing). These months also offer an opportunity for quiet, invigorating walks.

SPRING

Even early spring offers many plants and blossoms of interest: spring bedding in the Terrace and Summer Garden, the magnolias, the sight of the narcissus in the Alpine Meadow, and then the spectacular azaleas and rhododendrons.

MARCH

Battleston Hill camellias and magnolias, eg. *C.* × *williamsii* 'Donation', *M. kobus* var. *stellata*, *M.* 'Iolanthe'
Winter Garden early rhododendrons

Spring: The crocus bank on the Walled Garden side of Seven Acres

Alpine Houses alpines in abundance
Weather Hill the almond-scented blossom of *Oemleria (Osmaronia) cerasiformis*
Pinetum a representative collection of *Narcissus*
Howard's Field National Collection of *Erica*

APRIL

Battleston Hill camellias and magnolias
Fruit Field fruit blossom
Rock Garden gentians and countless other alpines
Alpine Meadow the spectacle of thousands of naturalised *Narcissus bulbocodium*
Formal Garden spring and summer bedding schemes
Wild Garden primulas and spring-flowering shrubs

MAY

Battleston Hill azaleas and rhododendrons; silverbell or snowdrop tree, *Halesia monticola* var. *vestita*
Rock Garden the rustic bridge over the Long Ponds, draped with *Wisteria floribunda* f. *macrobotrys*; rock garden plants
Formal Garden clematis on the south-facing wall and other wall shrubs and climbers
Canal Loggia framed by *Wisteria floribunda* f. *macrobotrys* and *W. venusta*
Seven Acres shrubs; herbaceous plants

SUMMER

Every area of the garden is full of vigour and interest in this season of such full-blown beauty. The Mixed Borders, the Summer Garden and roses are at their finest, the trials plants in the Portsmouth Field burst into colour and the Model Vegetable Garden produces a range of food crops.

JUNE

Terrace summer bedding plants
Weather Hill new English roses
The Portsmouth Field Trials, notably delphinium

Mediterranean Garden cistus; other sun-loving shrubs

Summer Garden (June onwards) tree peony, *Paeonia suffruticosa* 'Rock's Variety'; musk roses 'Buff Beauty' and 'Cornelia', *Rosa* 'Zéphirine Drouhin'

Garden for New Rose Introductions 200 cultivars of bush and pillar rose

Formal Garden on the south-facing wall, twining *Schisandra glaucescens* with orange-red flowers

JULY

Terrace summer bedding plants

Model Gardens

Rose Gardens Garden for New Rose Introductions; Rose Catenary and rose borders

Laboratory building borders

Canal water lilies; in south-facing border, mainly summer-flowering shrubs and perennials; hardy *Fuchsia magellanica*; double-flowered, *Hibiscus syriacus*

AUGUST

Model Gardens including Model Vegetable Garden

Fruit Field ripening fruit

Summer: in the Formal Garden standard fuchsias and heliotrope carry through a traditional planting scheme

Laboratory building trumpet vine, *Campsis* × *tagliabuana* 'Madame Galen'
Howard's Field *Erica cinerea*

AUTUMN

A season to delight the senses: the brilliant colours of exotic trees and shrubs, pungent smells, the perhaps unexpected flowering bulbs of the Alpine Meadow, and the sight and smell of fruit and vegetables being harvested.

SEPTEMBER

Autumn Borders (until Oct) chrysanthemums and asters; distinctive *Aster lateriflorus* 'Horizontalis', a bush of minute leaves and pale lilac flowers
Battleston Hill sprays of yellow shuttlecock flowers dangle from *Kirengeshoma palmata*; Japanese and Canadian maples; foliage of *Enkianthus campanulatus* and *Fothergilla major*

Autumn: *Liquidambar styraciflua* in Seven Acres

Fruit Field trees display ripe fruit
Laboratory building borders include the pink trumpets of belladonna lily, *Amaryllis belladonna*
Formal Garden *Celastrus*, with scarlet and gold seed capsules
Heather Garden *Calluna vulgaris* cultivars

OCTOBER

Autumn Borders Japanese anemones; *Sedum spectabile*; the violet-flowered *Liriope muscari*
Battleston Hill Japanese and Canadian maples
Howard's Field Heather Garden

Canal large specimen of *Parrotia persica*
Seven Acres *Nyssa sylvatica; Liquidambar styraciflua*

Winter: sun and ice on
a January day in the
Rose Catenary facing
the Bowes Lyon
Pavilion

NOVEMBER

Winter Garden
Glasshouses *Dendranthema* display
Alpine Houses alpines changed regularly
Pinetum

WINTER

A season of mist and stillness. Admire bark patterns, coloured
berries and tree shapes, listen to bird calls, and look for frosty
animal tracks. The welcoming colour and variety of displays in
the Alpine Houses and the Glasshouses provide warm inter-
ludes as will a stop at the Restaurant on the way to the Heather
Garden. Camellias and forsythia soon appear, as do snowdrops and cyclamen.

DECEMBER

Winter Garden (Nov-Mar) a variety of scented mahonias and
   sarcococcas

Glasshouses numerous exotic displays
Alpine Houses alpines changed regularly
Seven Acres trees and shrubs with coloured barks; *Hamamelis japonica, H. mollis*
Wild Garden hellebores

CREDITS

Written by Pat Pierce, with the assistance of Jim Gardiner, Curator, and other staff at Wisley

Maps by John Fitzmaurice

Designed by John Fitzmaurice & Neil Chapman

Typeset by SX Composing Ltd., Rayleigh, Essex

Printed by The KPC Group, London and Ashford, Kent

Photographs: RHS, Wisley with the exception of the following:
Jim Gardiner front flap, pp. 11, 18, 20, 55, 57 (bot), 62, 63;
John Glover pp 33, 35;
Andrew Lawson p. 29;
Peter K. Lloyd pp. 1, 47.

JANUARY

Conifer Lawn range of *Chamaecyparis lawsoniana* cultivars
Winter Garden (Jan-Mar) Chinese witch hazel; blossom of *Prunus subhirtella* 'Autumnalis'; gaily coloured berries of *Pernettya mucronata* 'Winter Time
Glasshouses numerous exotic displays
Alpine Houses *Crocus sieberi; C. chrysanthus* cultivars
Rock Garden cyclamen; snowdrops
Laboratory building White, heavily perfumed flowers of *Viburnum foetens*, facing the front door in the first alcove on the right; by the archway, elegant pink and white blooms of *Camellia japonica* 'Princess Charlotte'
Walled Garden the uncommon winter-flowering *Clematis napaulensis* with *Iris unguicularis* underneath
Seven Acres
Pinetum snake bark maples

FEBRUARY

Conifer Lawn Chilean incense cedar, *Austrocedrus (Libocedrus) chilensis*; rare *Juniperus monosperma* with feathery foliage
Winter Garden snaky-striped bark of *Acer grosseri* var. *hersii*
Glasshouses numerous exotic displays, notably orchids
Weather Hill crocus lawn behind Bowes Lyon Pavilion
Alpine Houses alpines changed regularly
Model Vegetable Garden winter lettuce
Rock Garden *Rhododendron* × *praecox*
Laboratory building scented *Daphne odora* in the beds
Walled Garden *Clematis cirrhosa* var. *balearica*
Wild Garden Lenten roses, *Helleborus orientalis*; witch hazels; *Narcissus cyclamineus*; snowdrops; snowflakes
Battleston Hill (mid-Feb) rhododendrons and azaleas begin; crocus; snowdrops; hellebores
Seven Acres crocus bank by Walled Garden